Simple Solutions™
Trailering

By Micaela Myers

Illustrations by Jean Abernethy

Plus tips for stress-free loading

BOWTIE
P R E S S®

A Division of BowTie, Inc.
Irvine, California

Karla Austin, *Director of Operations & Product Development*
Nick Clemente, *Special Consultant*
Barbara Kimmel, *Editor in Chief*
Jessica Knott, *Production Supervisor*
Amy Stirnkorb, *Designer*

The horses in this book are referred to as she and he in alternating chapters unless their sexes are apparent from the activity discussed.

Library of Congress Cataloging-in-Publication Data

Myers, Micaela, 1974–
 Trailering / by Micaela Myers ; illustrations by Jean Abernethy.
  p. cm. — (Horse illustrated simple solutions)
 ISBN 978-1-933958-06-4
 1. Horse trailers. I. Title.
 SF285.385.M94 2007
 636.1'083—dc22
          2007012755

BowTie Press®
A Division of BowTie, Inc.
3 Burroughs
Irvine, California 92618

Printed and bound in Singapore
16 15 14 13 12 11 10 09 08 07 1 2 3 4 5 6 7 8 9 10

CONTENTS

Matching Your Truck and Trailer

For the majority of horse owners, the number one concern in trailering is how to get the horse in the trailer. But discussing how to load your horse before making sure the trailer is safe for her puts the cart before the horse — or, rather, the horse before the trailer! A truck or an SUV plus a hitch does not necessarily equal a safe rig. If the tow vehicle or the hitch that connects vehicle and trailer is not rated to pull the load you're hauling, you're on a one-way road to disaster. So do your homework ahead of time, and make sure your truck, trailer, hitch, and horses are all a proper match.

The Trailer and Tow Vehicle

Before you bring your horse anywhere near your trailer, do some research and some basic calculations to be sure that your tow vehicle and trailer will not be overloaded and that your fully loaded (think passengers and gear) truck or SUV is rated to pull the weight of your fully loaded horse trailer. First, find the weight and loading information given by the manufacturers of your tow vehicle and trailer. This information should be listed on a label attached to the vehicle itself (usually in the driver's doorpost) or in the owner's manual.

Look for two figures: the gross vehicle weight rating (GVWR) and the vehicle's net weight, or base curb weight. The GVWR is the maximum weight that truck or trailer is designed to carry: the weight of the vehicle itself plus the hitch and kingpin, passengers, fluids, and cargo. The net, or base curb, weight measures only the standard vehicle with a full fuel tank. Subtract the net weight of each vehicle from its GVWR to find the total additional weight you may safely load into it.

Next, find your tow vehicle's tow rating, the maximum weight it can safely pull. To determine whether your fully loaded trailer is too much for your tow vehicle to handle, add the weight of your horses and gear to the net weight of the trailer. This is the trailer's gross vehicle weight (GVW). If the GVW is under both your tow vehicle's tow rating and your trailer's GVWR, you should be OK. Many vehicle manufacturers also provide additional towing information, such as the kingpin load (see "The Trailer and Hitch") and how much rear gross axle weight the truck or SUV can handle, to help you determine whether your rig falls within safe limits.

If you aren't buying a new trailer and you do not have your trailer's weight information, you can weigh the trailer at a drive-on public scale. The weight information is critical. If you try to haul a load heavier than the weight your tow vehicle is rated for, you'll have trouble accelerating and stopping, you'll wear out your tow vehicle quickly, and you could cause a serious accident, so don't take any chances.

The Trailer and Hitch

There are two basic types of trailer: tag-along and gooseneck. Tag-along trailers are hitched behind the tow vehicle; gooseneck

Gooseneck Trailer

Tag-along Trailer

trailers are hitched inside the truck bed. Many trucks and SUVs come equipped with hitches, but that doesn't mean the components of the hitch are rated for the load you plan to haul. All hitch components, including the ball and the slide-in ball mount, must be the correct size and must be rated to pull the fully loaded weight of your trailer.

Tag-along trailers (also called bumper pull trailers) require a professionally installed hitch, rated Class III or higher, attached to the frame of the vehicle. Although tag-along trailers are sometimes called bumper pull, never pull a tag-along by connecting it directly to your bumper; always use a hitch. Hitches have two weight ratings—one for the weight the hitch can bear without additional support, and a higher figure for the weight it can

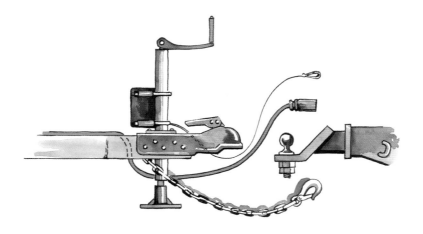

handle if it is equipped with weight distribution bars. Weight distribution bars are add-ons that distribute the weight of the trailer to all axels of the tow vehicle, often improving handling as well as stability. Check the hitch weight ratings to determine whether

you need to pur-
chase weight distrib-
ution bars. If so,
you'll probably want
to have them profes-
sionally installed.

Gooseneck trail-
ers feature a ball
hitch mounted in the

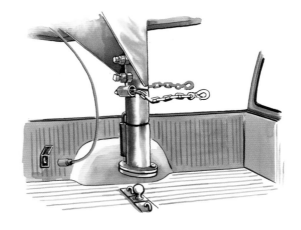

bed of the pickup truck. The ball component in the truck bed fits
into the coupler component on the overlapping section of the
trailer. This hitch also must be professionally installed and rated
for the load you plan to haul. The kingpin load listed on the

weight distribution label or in the owners' manual is the amount of weight that can be placed on the hitch.

Whether you pull a tag-along or a gooseneck, check that you have the exact size ball you need for your coupler. A difference of even a fraction of an inch could mean your trailer won't attach snugly or could bounce off. And when your trailer is attached to your tow vehicle, make sure it is perfectly level at all times. For tag-along trailers, slide-in ball mounts can be purchased with varying drops (that can also be turned upside down into lifts) to make your trailer attach level. A trailer that tips forward or back puts stress on the hitch, forces your horse to work harder to keep her balance, causes uneven tire wear, and makes the ride bumpier and more dangerous.

Choosing a Trailer

If you don't already have a trailer and wish to purchase one, be an informed buyer. Horse trailers come in a wide variety of sizes, materials, and styles with a seemingly endless choice of features. With a little preparation, you can narrow your search for a trailer that fits your needs and budget and makes the hauling experience safe and comfortable for you and your horse. Here are a few key points to consider:

Size: You must choose a trailer that is wide enough and tall enough for the largest horse you may haul. Your horse should be able to raise his head without danger of hitting the ceiling, and he needs enough room both side-to-side and front-to-back to shift his weight to balance during turns and stops. Although size varies by manufacturer, trailer models labeled standard size are typically about seven feet high and a minimum of six feet wide; extra-large models are wider and taller by several inches. Many manufacturers will indicate what size horse the trailer is

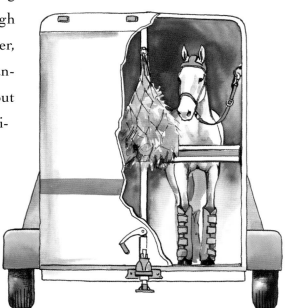

Straight Load Trailer

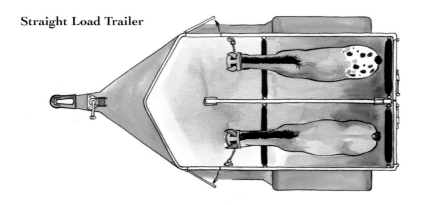

designed to accommodate. And all trailers are sized to haul a specific number of horses, from the smallest one-horse model to huge fifteen-horse vans.

Style: Both tag-along and gooseneck trailers come in a variety of styles: straight load, in which the horses walk straight in and

Slant Load Trailer

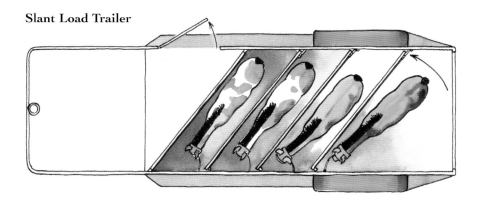

ride facing forward; slant load, in which the horses stand diagonally; and stock, in which there are no dividers between horses and which has slatted rather than solid sides. Some trailers add length for dressing rooms, tack compartments, or sleeping quarters. Trailers are made of aluminum or steel or various combinations of metal, wood, and synthetic materials such as phenolic resin or fiberglass. Each material has advantages and disadvantages. For example, steel is heavier and can rust but is far cheaper than aluminum; reinforced fiberglass is lighter and quieter than aluminum in trailer roofs but not as "horseproof" in structural panels.

Carefully consider which trailer style will best fit the weight limits of your tow vehicle, the size of your horses, and your intended use. How heavy or light your trailer use will be depends on how many horses you haul, how often you haul them, and whether your trips are primarily day trips or long-distance overnight journeys. If you are considering a stock trailer, keep in mind that if you're hauling in cold weather, the semi-open sides can make the interior chilly for horses.

Condition: Whether you already own a trailer or are considering a used one, thoroughly check its condition. Structural parts such as doors and floors must be sound and in good working order, or they should be replaced. Any rust should be only surface deep, not impairing the integrity of the trailer's structure.

Mats: Whether the trailer floor is made of wood or aluminum, nonslip mats are essential; they help protect the floor and make the ride much more comfortable for the horse.

Brakes: A horse trailer needs its own set of brakes. Trailer brakes not only save your tow vehicle brakes but also help keep the trailer from jackknifing, and in most states they are required by law. Most trailer brakes are electric; when you hitch your trailer, its electric lines plug into the tow vehicle, and the trailer brakes and taillights are activated when the driver presses the brake pedal. Generally, a trailer brake control box is installed inside the tow vehicle as well, within easy reach of the driver. Sensors in the control box can be adjusted to vary the brake force and to calibrate the trailer brakes to activate slightly before the tow vehicle's brakes. A lever on the control box also allows the driver to manually activate the trailer brake, when necessary, without stepping on the tow vehicle's brake pedal; this is the right way to get control of a trailer that begins to sway.

Trailers also need an emergency brake called a breakaway brake. This battery-powered device, located on the trailer coupler, is connected to the tow vehicle by a cable. If the trailer somehow pulls free from the tow vehicle and the cable is disconnected,

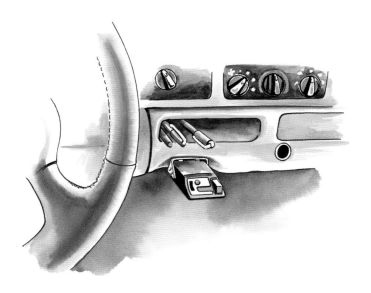

the breakaway battery will engage the trailer brakes and bring
the runaway trailer to a stop.

Ventilation: Trailers can get very hot or very cold inside, depending on the outside temperature. In any weather, it's imperative that your horse trailer be adequately ventilated and that your horses have plenty of fresh air. Never let your horse hang his head outside the trailer, however. Barred or screened windows and ceiling vents should allow fresh air to circulate freely, and trailer fans can be installed to increase the airflow in hot weather.

Suspension: If you haul often or over long distances, your horse's ride will be less stressful if you buy a trailer with good suspension or upgrade your current trailer.

Hooking Up and Driving

Improperly attached trailers and careless driving are two major causes of hauling accidents. You no doubt consider your horses precious cargo, so hook up and drive your rig with careful consideration and due vigilance. Your horses are depending on you.

Hooking Up

Every time you hook up your trailer, perform each step in the sequence in the same order, and always double-check your work. When you follow the same order each time, you are less likely to forget steps, which can give you additional peace of mind while traveling to your destination. Here is an example:

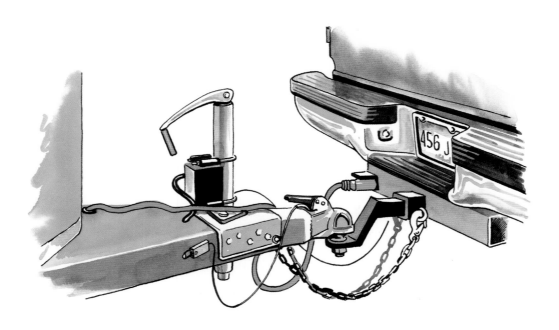

1. Secure the receiver or coupler on the hitch ball.

2. Attach the safety chains, which should be crossed, left chain to right side, right chain to left side (the chains must clip, not simply hook, to the tow vehicle).

3. Adjust the length of the safety chains. They should be long enough to allow the vehicle to turn without engaging the chains, but not so loose that they drag on the ground for tag-along trailers.

4. Attach the trailer brakes (including the safety) and the electrics.

5. Make sure the trailer is level.

6. Check that the trailer brakes and taillights work and are properly adjusted.

Driving

It is illegal for humans to ride in horse trailers on the road, but if you have a chance to take a jaunt in one down your driveway, you'll learn what a rocky ride your horse endures. Always keep this in mind when you drive, and follow these general rules:

- Never go above the speed limit.
- Double the following distance that is recommended for a passenger car.
- Brake slowly.
- Take turns cautiously.
- Don't talk on your cell phone while driving.
- Know your route to avoid or at least anticipate dangers, such as raised railroad tracks.

- Whenever possible, avoid hauling your horse and trailer during rush hour; heavy traffic means more stop-and-go handling, a longer journey, and more stress for both you and your horse.

If you are new to pulling a trailer or have recently purchased a new model, practice driving with the trailer attached so you can sharpen your skills and build your confidence. Find a large vacant parking lot, and practice turning and backing your rig into parking spaces. For an added challenge, place orange traffic cones in the lot, and practice turning around them and backing between them. Get used to your rig's turning radius so you'll be able to judge whether you have enough room to turn around in a space before you enter it.

Preloading Training

People expect to spend weeks and often months training their horses to do many things, such as working on longe line or taking the correct lead. Yet, when it comes to trailer loading, many horse owners walk their horses to a trailer and expect them to go in willingly. But to a horse, walking into a trailer is unnatural behavior. Horses are prey animals; they rely on their ability to run away from danger and instinctively fear places they can't run from. Horse trailers are small, dark, confined spaces, exactly the kind of spaces that horses are naturally wary of entering. If the horse balks, too often the handler forces him in—ensuring that future loading sessions will be all the more frightening to the horse.

This bad experience can be avoided if you begin trailer loading training many weeks or even months before you need to go anywhere. Done right, the end result is a willing, calm horse that will load every time you ask him. Before introducing your horse to the trailer, make sure he has the skills he needs to load and unload safely and successfully.

Leading

First and foremost, your horse must have good basic ground manners. He should whoa and walk or move forward on command, with a verbal cue. For your training sessions, make sure that your horse is outfitted in a properly fitted halter and a sturdy cotton lead rope. If your horse tends to be reluctant to move forward when you ask, carry a long whip such as a dressage whip.

Verbally ask your horse to walk. If he doesn't respond, begin walking forward, gently pulling the lead rope as you go. If he still doesn't move forward, tap him on his rear end with the dressage whip, moving forward as you do. Follow the steps of ask (say "walk"), tell (pull forward on the lead rope), and reinforce (tap with the whip) until your horse moves forward with the verbal cue alone.

For horses that do not stop when you give the verbal command *whoa*, pull back on the lead rope and cease forward motion. If the horse still doesn't stop, release pressure on the lead rope, then pull down and back sharply, repeating if necessary. The minute the horse stops, even for a moment, ask him to back up several steps (see "Backing" below). Follow this ask-tell-reinforce routine until the horse learns to stop with the verbal command *whoa*.

Backing

Backing is another important skill. Even if your horse can turn around in your trailer and won't need to back out, backing on command is a good skill for him to have. If he must be hauled by someone else in an emergency situation and the trailer happens to be a straight load, he'll need to be able to back out safely. Plus, backing comes in handy in any number of handling situations, such as during grooming or handling in a confined space.

Your goal is for your horse to back with a verbal command, such as *back*; achieving this goal takes practice and training. Start by asking your horse to back with the verbal command, followed by pulling the lead rope toward his chest, which will put pressure on his nose. If he still refuses to walk back, pull the lead rope toward his chest with your left hand while you press his left shoulder back with your right hand. At first, reward even one step back with a pat and praise. Continue to ask, then tell, then reinforce (with the push) until your horse learns to respond to the verbal cue alone.

Keep your backing sessions short, practicing every day for a few minutes until your horse backs six or seven feet easily and in a straight line with just a verbal cue. This may take several weeks. Once your horse is successful, add to the challenge by walking your horse between two ground poles (round poles several inches in diameter and several feet long, laid parallel on the ground) and then asking him to back through them. Start with the poles far apart, and

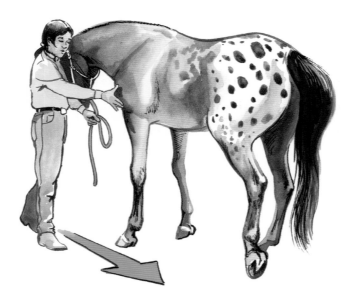

gradually work them closer together until the distance between them equals the width of a straight load trailer compartment.

Stepping Up

When your horse walks into the trailer, he must step up either onto a ramp or into the trailer and onto a foreign footing, usually a wood or aluminum floor covered with mats. Prepare him for this task by working on a trail-course bridge, such as one designed for trail classes at horse shows. These bridges are rectangular—several feet long by several feet wide—and are raised a few inches off the ground. If you don't have access to a trail-course bridge, you can build your own or simulate one by laying a sturdy flat board on the ground.

First, walk your horse up to the bridge and let him smell it, then ask him to take a step forward. This is the same technique you will soon use for trailer loading. Don't put constant pressure on the lead rope; remember that he should walk forward with a verbal command. Once he willingly puts one foot on the bridge, ask him to whoa in that position, praise him, and then ask him to back off the bridge. Work your way up to two feet on and off the

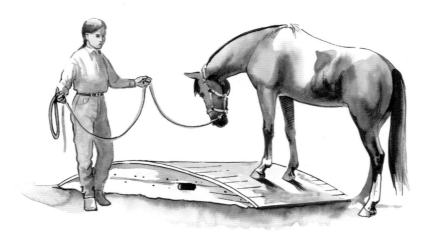

bridge, and ultimately to all the way on and off. Walking forward, stopping, and backing off reinforces your horse's understanding that he should listen to you and take his time. Many horses run backward or forward out of trailers and hurt themselves in their panic to escape. Teach your horse to take his time entering and exiting. With some trailers, you will not be able to walk in beside your horse, and he will need to walk forward without you actively leading him, so you may want to practice sending your horse all the way over the bridge while you stand to the side.

Tying

Even if you don't tie your horse in the trailer, he should be capable of standing quietly tied for long periods of time (twenty minutes or more, under supervision). Always make sure he's tied with a quick-release knot or snap to something he cannot pull down. He should be tied at withers' height or higher at a length at which he can hold his head naturally without getting tangled

in the rope. Never reward your horse with freedom or treats if he paws or wiggles when tied. A horse that's properly trained to tie should stand still for grooming and while you work nearby cleaning your tack or his pen.

Introducing the Trailer

Once your horse has solid skills—he reliably responds to your forward, whoa, and backing cues; ties well; and willingly enters places with ceilings, such as barns and shelters—you can introduce him to the trailer. At first, let him become familiar with the trailer without any intention of loading him. Let him walk around it and smell it. Open the back doors and secure them so he can look inside and smell the mats. Put a treat inside, or some hay in a hay bag or a manger, so the trailer smells good to him. Praise him as he investigates, and repeat this activity for several days before your first loading session.

Get your horse used to wearing shipping boots and a head bumper during the weeks leading up to your first loading session.

With the proper preparation, you're ready to hook up the trailer and begin your loading lessons.

Loading the Horse

For your first loading session, make sure your trailer is hooked up to the tow vehicle and is parked on a level surface with plenty of room around the trailer. Never load your horse into a trailer that is not hooked up to the tow vehicle: unhitched trailers are very unstable and can easily roll forward or back. You may wish to place wheel chocks on the trailer tires for added stability. Secure the trailer doors wide open, and open any trailer windows. Place hay in the bags or mangers, and outfit your horse in shipping boots and a head bumper for safety.

Your horse should already be familiar with the sight and smell of the trailer from your preparatory work. Now it's time to ask

her to take her first steps in. Whether you can walk with your horse into the trailer depends on whether there's enough room for you to exit safely. This may be possible in a large slant load or a stock trailer, or in a smaller trailer with an escape door; however, keep in mind that entering any confined space with a horse is dangerous. In two-horse straight loads, you may be able to walk in on the other side of the divider from your horse. Choose your strategy ahead of time, with safety in mind, and never let yourself be pinned in the trailer with your horse between you and the exit.

During the loading process, avoid standing in front of your horse or facing her, and don't get in a tug-of-war—you'll lose! If you've done your homework, your horse should willingly walk forward on command. Let her take her time. At first, ask for only one foot on the ramp or into the trailer if it's a step-up type. Then praise her. If she seems nervous, ask her to back out of the trailer. In this way, as in preloading training, your horse learns to obey you and not rush in or out. If she's calm and not rushing, and if she is willing, let her walk all the way in. If she isn't willing to go that far during your first session, try to at least work your horse up to putting both front feet on the ramp or into the trailer and then backing off willingly and repeating.

In the subsequent loading sessions, work your way up to walking your horse calmly all the way into the trailer, praising her, letting her stand for a moment, and then backing out. Always encourage her to back out slowly, with your voice command, one step at a time.

If at any point your horse begins to show resistance to trailer loading by refusing to move forward, backing away from the trailer, or moving sideways, put her to work nearby. There should be plenty of room around the trailer, so take her several feet away and reinforce your groundwork. Ask her to walk in a circle, back up in a straight line, stop and then walk on, and so on. Groundwork exercises will get her mind off the trailer and reinforce her obedience. After a few minutes of drills, reapproach the trailer and try loading again.

Keep your trailer-loading sessions short—five to twenty minutes each day. When your horse will willingly walk in and stand in the trailer for several minutes, calmly munching food, get her used to the sounds and sights of the doors and windows opening and closing. Practice securing the butt bar and closing the trailer door while your horse stands inside for a minute or two. But never stand behind a loaded horse, as you never know when she'll decide to bolt out. Afterward, open things up, back her out, and praise her. When your horse is comfortable standing in the closed trailer for five minutes or so, she's probably ready for you to take her on a short drive. Don't go far—a five- to ten-minute drive is long enough—and avoid sharp turns. Repeat this a number of times, adding a few minutes to each outing.

Although you want your horse to be comfortable loading on either side of a straight load trailer, for traveling, always haul a single horse or the heaviest horse on the left side to help balance the trailer and accommodate the rise in the middle of most roads.

For slant load trailers, haul the heaviest horse or a single horse in the front position.

The process of teaching your horse to load may seem time consuming, but it's worth the investment. A horse that's been properly trained to load, unload, and travel will be a pleasure to take places and less likely to injure herself in the process.

Trailer Maintenance and Upkeep

Although most people reliably service their tow vehicle every 3,000 miles, many forget to ever service their horse trailer! Your horse trailer should be serviced by a professional at least once a year. At that time, the axels should be serviced and the trailer wiring inspected.

The floor and body of the trailer should also be regularly inspected for and wear and tear. Any rusted areas should be quickly attended to before they cause body damage. Grease or soap the ball of the trailer hitch regularly to prevent squeaking and rubbing from the hitch ball receiver. Door hinges also benefit from regular lubrication.

Even if your trailer is parked on level ground, always use wheel chocks to properly secure it from rolling. Store your trailer in a garage or under a shelter, if possible. If shelter is not available, consider using a trailer cover. Sitting in the sun and bearing the full weight of the horse trailer day in and day out can quickly wear out tires. If your trailer will be stored for long stretches of time, raise the vehicle on blocks and use tire covers.

Replace trailer tires every three to five years. Don't let tread alone dictate when you replace your trailer tires; because many trailers don't travel long distances, sidewall cracking may occur before tread wears thin. Check the tires, including the spare, for optimum inflation at least once a month, and always purchase trailer tires rated to handle your fully loaded rig.

Healthy Horse Transit

Traveling can take its toll on your horse, so it's important that you do everything you can to reduce stress and minimize the risk of injury or illness. Here are a few tips for keeping your horse healthy and happy and arriving at your destination safely:

To tie or not to tie: Whether you tie your horse in the trailer or not depends on your particular horse and trailer. The advantages of leaving your horse untied, if circumstances allow, are that she can lower her head to clear her lungs and has more freedom of movement for balance. If your horse is in danger of wiggling into a dangerous position or fighting with another horse, it may be best to tie her during her trailer ride. Don't leave your horse's lead rope on; it is too long and could entangle her in the event of an accident. Instead, use a tie strap with a quick release snap, which is also easier to undo in an emergency. Attach the quick release end to the trailer tie ring, and adjust

the strap so that your horse can move her head comfortably but can't get into trouble.

Feed: If you choose to feed your horse in transit, reduce dust by soaking the hay ahead of time. In certain trailer models, you can place hay on the floor; other trailers have mangers. Hay bags are also an option, but attach them high enough that your horse can't get a leg caught in them.

Bedding: Although thick nonslip rubber mats make bedding unnecessary, bedding may encourage your horse to pee because the urine won't splash your horse the way it does on rubber mats. Pick a low-dust product, and concentrate it where the urine will fall.

Long trips: On long trips, stop at least every four hours. Balancing in a moving trailer is hard work for a horse, and regular breaks are important. If your horse will eat, drink water offered to her, and poop and pee in the trailer, you do not need to unload her. If she will not—many horses will not drink in the trailer—she must be unloaded. If you must unload your horse, pick a safe place to stop ahead of time, and make sure you've done your homework so she'll reload easily. Don't let her eat grass when you stop because you don't know if it's been treated with pesticides. Pack water from home, as horses often don't like the taste of strange water.

If your journey will take more than eight hours, you probably should arrange to stop for the night. There are a number of publications and Web sites to help you find overnight stabling, including:

http://www.overnightstabling.com

http://www.horsetrip.com

http://www.horsemotel.com

http://www.bbonline.com

Kits: Always travel with a first aid kit for your horse and a fully stocked automobile emergency kit that includes flares, jumper cables, a flashlight, and tools. Add a trailer jack and wheel chocks as a precaution.

Breakdown: Flat tires are likely the most common cause of a breakdown. Don't try to change a trailer's flat tire yourself. If possible, drive slowly to the nearest service station, and let a professional do the job: wheel nuts and bolts must be properly torqued, and it's not safe to unload your horse on the side of a road.

Have an emergency plan in case your vehicle breaks down, even if you can reach a service station. Always carry important phone numbers, including numbers for your veterinarian, farrier, and friends who have trailers and tow rigs in case you become stranded. Most automobile clubs will not tow a horse trailer with live cargo, so check the limitations of your membership. USRider is a roadside assistance provider for equestrians that offers services including trailer towing and both veterinarian and farrier locators.

With a little planning and good equipment, you can safely hit the open road with your horse. Done right, both of you will enjoy exploring new destinations. Happy travels!

About the Author

Micaela Myers has an MFA in writing and is the author of *The Horse Illustrated Guide to Trail Riding*. She has owned horses for twenty-five years, regularly trailering them to horse shows and campouts. Micaela currently owns a historic 1940 single-horse trailer, which she successfully taught her various horses and ponies to willingly load into.